▸ THIS JOURNAL BELONGS TO ◂

THE POWER OF HABIT

Habits aren't destiny. Habits can be ignored, changed, or replaced. But the difficult thing about the science of habits and the research behind it is that most people want to know the secret formula for quickly changing any habit. If scientists have discovered how these patterns work, then it stands to reason that they must have also found a recipe for rapid change, right? If only it were that easy.

Individuals and habits are all different, and so the specifics of diagnosing and changing the patterns in our lives differ from person to person and behavior to behavior. Giving up cigarettes is different from changing how you communicate with your spouse, which is different from how you prioritize tasks at work. What's more, each person's habits are driven by different cravings.

There isn't one prescription or secret formula because there are thousands. But inside this planner, you'll find a framework for understanding how your habits work and a guide to experimenting with how they might change. Some habits will be easy to analyze and influence, while others are more complex and require prolonged study.

This planner will help you easily distill the tactics that researchers have found for diagnosing and shaping the habits in your life. It offers a practical guide, and paired with a year of experimentation and self-reflection, it'll help with where to go next. Change might not be fast, and it isn't always easy. But with time and effort, almost any habit can be reshaped.

It's time to change your life.

THE FRAMEWORK

 Identify the routine    Isolate the cue

 Experiment with rewards    Have a plan

STEP 1: IDENTIFY THE ROUTINE

MIT researchers have discovered a simple neurological loop at the core of every habit, a loop that consists of three parts: a **cue**, a **routine**, and a **reward**.

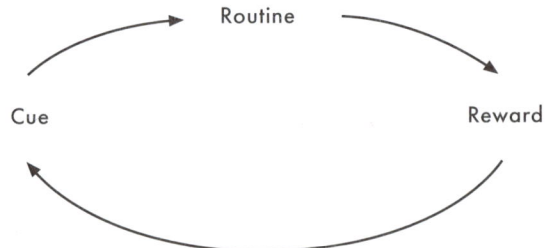

First, there's a **cue,** a trigger that makes the behavior unfold automatically. Studies tell us that a cue can be a location, time of day, certain emotional state, other people, or a pattern of behaviors that consistently triggers a certain routine.

The next part of the habit loop is the **routine**—the behavior or habit that you want to change.

Finally, the last part of the habit loop is the **reward**. In some respects, the reward is the most important part. Habits exist so that we can get the rewards that we want. But figuring out a reward is kind of tricky—and it may surprise you.

To understand your own habits, you need to identify these three components. Once you have diagnosed the habit loop of a particular behavior, you can look for ways to replace old vices with new routines.

As an example, let's say you have a bad habit, like going to the cafeteria and buying a chocolate chip cookie every afternoon. Let's say this habit has caused you to gain a few pounds. You've tried to force yourself to stop, but every afternoon you repeat the same routine. Tomorrow, you promise yourself, you'll muster the willpower to resist. But tomorrow the habit takes hold again.

How do you start diagnosing and then changing this behavior? By figuring out the habit loop. And the first step is to identify the **routine**. In this cookie scenario—as with most habits—the routine is the most obvious aspect: It's the behavior you want to change. Your routine is that you get up from your desk in the afternoon, walk to the cafeteria, buy a chocolate chip cookie, and eat it while chatting with friends. So that's what you put into the loop:

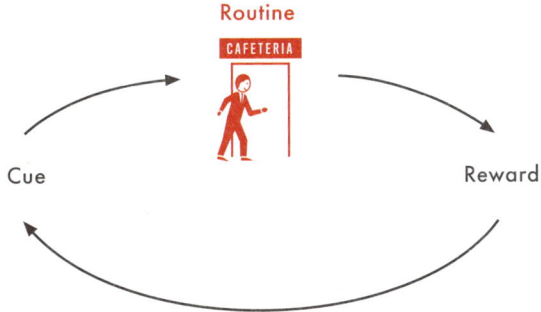

Next, some less obvious questions: What's the cue for this routine? Is it hunger? Boredom? Low blood sugar? That you need a break before plunging into another task?

And what's the reward? The cookie itself? The change of scenery? The temporary distraction? Socializing with colleagues? Or the burst of energy that comes from that blast of sugar? To figure this out, you'll need to do a little experimentation.

🚩 STEP 2: EXPERIMENT WITH REWARDS

Rewards are powerful because they satisfy cravings. But we're often not conscious of the cravings that drive our behaviors. Most cravings are obvious in retrospect, but incredibly hard to see when we are under their sway.

To figure out which cravings are driving particular habits, it's useful to experiment with different rewards. This might take a few days, or a week, or longer. During that period, you shouldn't feel any pressure to make a real change—think of yourself as a scientist in the data collection stage.

On the first day of your experiment, when you feel the urge to go to the cafeteria and buy a cookie, adjust your routine so it delivers a different reward. For instance, instead of walking to the cafeteria, go outside, walk around the block, and then go back to your desk without eating anything. The next day, go to the cafeteria and buy a donut, or a candy bar, and eat it at your desk. The day after that, instead of going to the cafeteria, walk over to your friend's office and gossip for a few minutes.

You get the idea. What you choose to do *instead* of buying a cookie isn't important. The point is to test different hypotheses to determine which craving is driving your routine. Are you craving the cookie itself, or a break from work? If it's the cookie, is it because you're hungry? (In which case an apple should work just as well.) Or are you wandering up to the cafeteria as an excuse to socialize, and the cookie is just a convenient excuse? (If so, walking to someone's desk and talking for a few minutes should satisfy the urge.)

As you test a few different rewards, you can use an old trick to look for patterns: After each activity, jot down the first three things that come to mind. They can be emotions, random thoughts, reactions on how you're feeling, or just the first three words that pop into your head.

Then, set an alarm on your watch or computer for fifteen minutes. When it goes off, ask yourself: Do you still feel the urge for that cookie?

The reason why it's important to write down three things—even if they are meaningless words—is twofold. First, it forces a momentary awareness of what you are thinking or feeling. What's more, studies show that writing down a few words helps in later recalling what you were thinking at that moment.

And why the fifteen-minute alarm? Because the point of these tests is to determine the reward you're craving. If, fifteen minutes after eating a donut, you *still* feel an urge to get up and go to the cafeteria, then your habit isn't motivated by a sugar craving. If, after gossiping at a colleague's desk, you still want a cookie, then the need for human contact isn't what's driving your behavior. On the other hand, if fifteen minutes after chatting with a friend, you find it easy to get back to work, then you've identified the reward—temporary distraction and socialization—that your habit sought to satisfy.

By experimenting with different rewards, you can isolate what you are *actually* craving, which is essential in redesigning the habit. In this example, after experimenting with rewards for a couple of days, you may realize that your reward has nothing to do with the cookie, but in fact, has to do with taking a break and socializing with friends.

Once you've figured out the routine and the reward, what remains is identifying the cue.

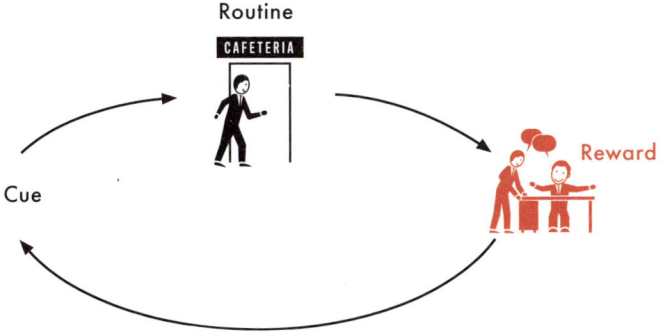

STEP 3: ISOLATE THE CUE

The reason why it is so hard to identify the cues that trigger our habits is because there is too much information bombarding us as our behaviors unfold. Ask yourself, do you eat breakfast at a certain time each day because you are hungry? Or because the clock says 7:30? Or because you're dressed, that's when the breakfast habit kicks in?

To identify a cue amid the noise, we can identify categories of behaviors ahead of time in order to see patterns. Luckily, science offers some help in this regard. Experiments have shown that almost all habitual cues fit into one of five categories. So if you're trying to figure out the cue for the "going to the cafeteria and buying a chocolate chip cookie" habit, you write down these five things the moment the urge hits.

Location

Time

Emotional state (how are you feeling?)

Other people (who else is around?)

Immediately preceding action (what were you doing when the urge hit?)

By taking note of these habitual clues, it will become clear which cue is triggering your cookie habit. For example, perhaps after a few days you narrowed down that every day between 3:00 and 4:00 in the afternoon, you felt the urge to go to the cafeteria and buy a cookie. You had already figured out that it wasn't hunger driving your behavior. The reward you were seeking was temporary distraction and socialization—the kind that comes from gossiping with a friend. Now you know what is triggering your habit is a certain time of day.

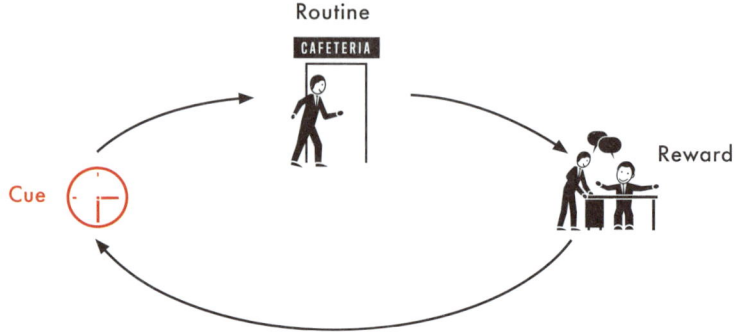

☑ STEP 4: HAVE A PLAN

Now, what you need is a plan. You've figured out your habit loop—the reward driving your behavior, the cue triggering it, and the routine itself—and now you can begin to shift the behavior. You can change to a better routine by planning for the cue and choosing a behavior that delivers the reward you are craving.

A habit is a formula our brain automatically follows: When I see CUE, I will do ROUTINE in order to get a REWARD. To re-engineer that formula, we need to begin making choices again. Take, for instance, the cookie-in-the-afternoon habit. Using the information, you can then write a plan to help you:

> AT 3:30, EVERY DAY, I WILL WALK TO A FRIEND'S DESK AND TALK FOR 10 MINUTES. TO MAKE SURE I REMEMBER TO DO THIS, I WILL SET THE ALARM ON MY WATCH FOR 3:30.

It might not work immediately. But on the days where you abide by your plan—when you walk to a friend's desk and chat for ten minutes—you might find yourself feeling better. Eventually, it will become automatic. After a few weeks, you might hardly think about the old routine anymore.

It will have become a habit.

This framework is a place to start. Sometimes change takes a long time. Sometimes it requires repeated experiments and failures. But once you understand how a habit operates—once you diagnose the cue, the routine, and the reward—you gain power over it.

So what are the cues, routines, and rewards in your life? **What habits do you want to change?**

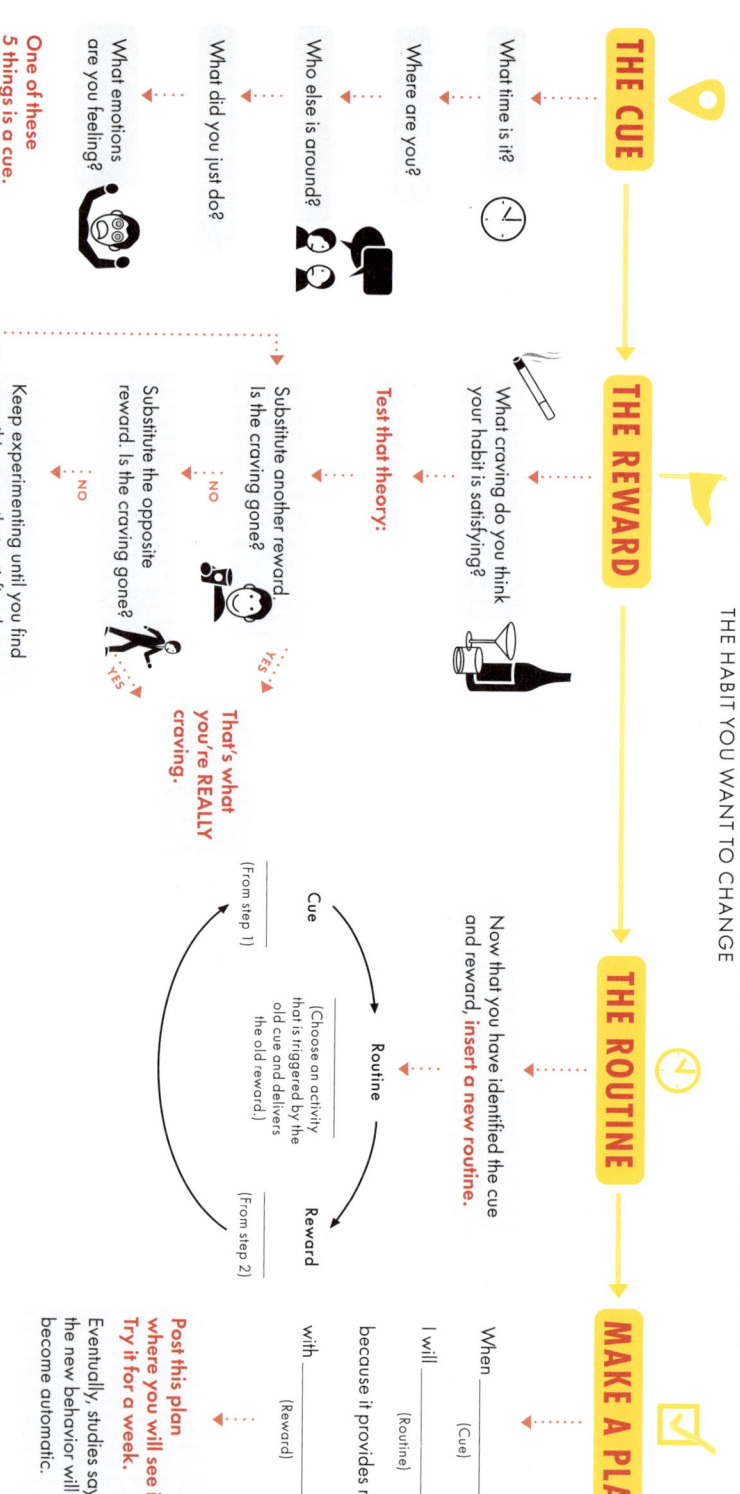

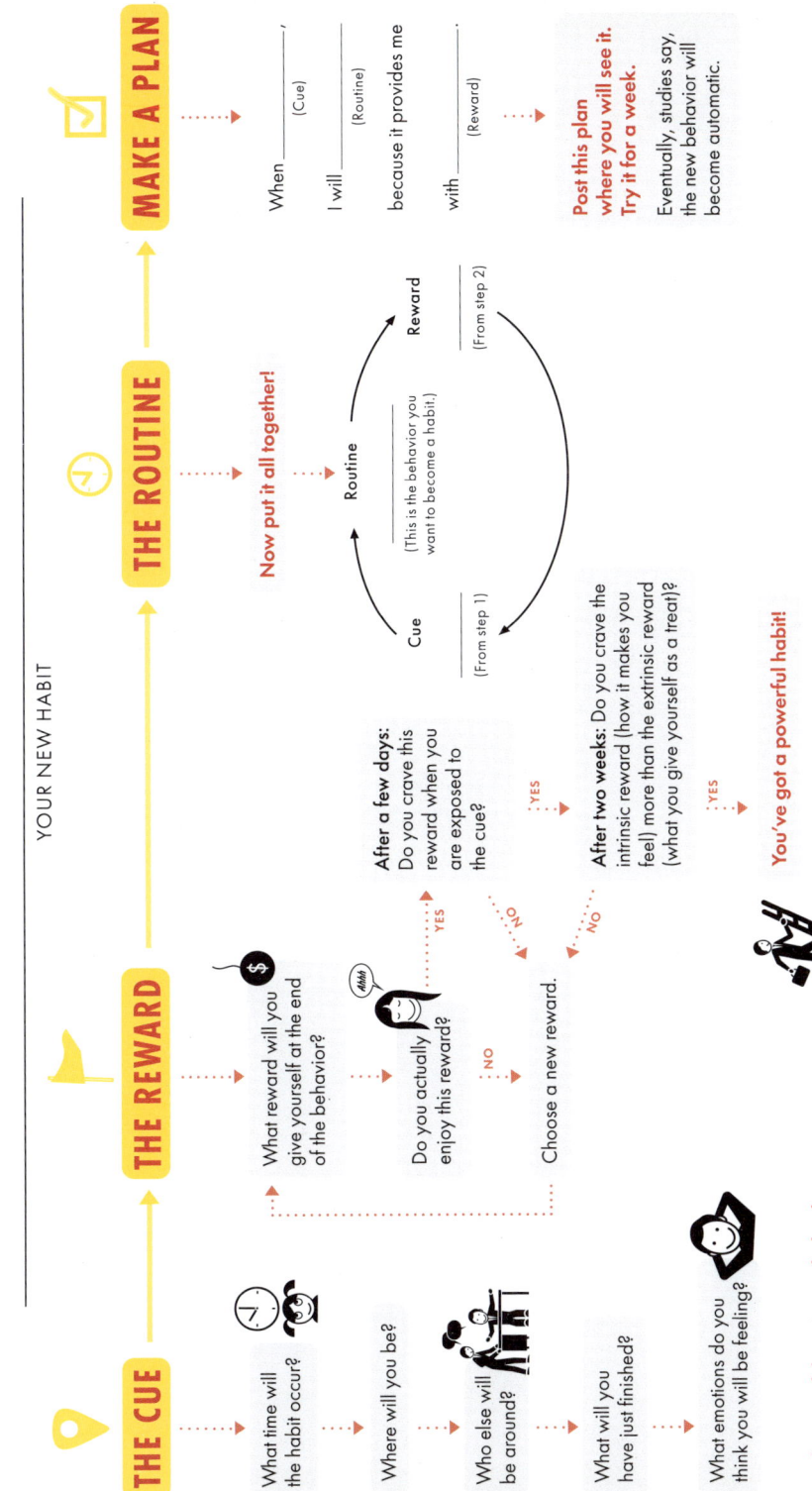

GOALS FOR THE YEAR

Now that we know a little bit more about habits, it's time to focus on YOU. The best way to change your habits is to be intentional—you have to *want* to make a change. What are your goals for the year?

What were you hoping to achieve by picking up this planner?

What positive changes do you want to create in your life?

After you've had some time to reflect, try to identify the specific habits you would like to work on this year. As you learned above, some habits might be really easy to change, others might not be. Don't try to take on too much! At most, I recommend only tackling and experimenting with one new habit every month. However, some habits that are more complex and ingrained in your everyday life may take more time. Give yourself the flexibility of one, two, or even three months to fully experiment with a tough habit in order to create positive change. Remember that you can always add to and change your list over the course of the year!

Habits to work on:

By transforming these goals into a plan and tracking these habits every month, you will start to see changes in your everyday life!

2022 AT A GLANCE

JANUARY 2022
S	M	T	W	T	F	S
						1
2	3	4	5	6	7	8
9	10	11	12	13	14	15
16	17	18	19	20	21	22
23/30	24/31	25	26	27	28	29

FEBRUARY 2022
S	M	T	W	T	F	S
		1	2	3	4	5
6	7	8	9	10	11	12
13	14	15	16	17	18	19
20	21	22	23	24	25	26
27	28					

MARCH 2022
S	M	T	W	T	F	S
		1	2	3	4	5
6	7	8	9	10	11	12
13	14	15	16	17	18	19
20	21	22	23	24	25	26
27	28	29	30	31		

APRIL 2022
S	M	T	W	T	F	S
					1	2
3	4	5	6	7	8	9
10	11	12	13	14	15	16
17	18	19	20	21	22	23
24	25	26	27	28	29	30

MAY 2022
S	M	T	W	T	F	S
1	2	3	4	5	6	7
8	9	10	11	12	13	14
15	16	17	18	19	20	21
22	23	24	25	26	27	28
29	30	31				

JUNE 2022
S	M	T	W	T	F	S
			1	2	3	4
5	6	7	8	9	10	11
12	13	14	15	16	17	18
19	20	21	22	23	24	25
26	27	28	29	30		

JULY 2022
S	M	T	W	T	F	S
					1	2
3	4	5	6	7	8	9
10	11	12	13	14	15	16
17	18	19	20	21	22	23
24/31	25	26	27	28	29	30

AUGUST 2022
S	M	T	W	T	F	S
	1	2	3	4	5	6
7	8	9	10	11	12	13
14	15	16	17	18	19	20
21	22	23	24	25	26	27
28	29	30	31			

SEPTEMBER 2022
S	M	T	W	T	F	S
				1	2	3
4	5	6	7	8	9	10
11	12	13	14	15	16	17
18	19	20	21	22	23	24
25	26	27	28	29	30	

OCTOBER 2022
S	M	T	W	T	F	S
						1
2	3	4	5	6	7	8
9	10	11	12	13	14	15
16	17	18	19	20	21	22
23/30	24/31	25	26	27	28	29

NOVEMBER 2022
S	M	T	W	T	F	S
		1	2	3	4	5
6	7	8	9	10	11	12
13	14	15	16	17	18	19
20	21	22	23	24	25	26
27	28	29	30			

DECEMBER 2022
S	M	T	W	T	F	S
				1	2	3
4	5	6	7	8	9	10
11	12	13	14	15	16	17
18	19	20	21	22	23	24
25	26	27	28	29	30	31

2023 AT A GLANCE

JANUARY 2023

S	M	T	W	T	F	S
1	2	3	4	5	6	7
8	9	10	11	12	13	14
15	16	17	18	19	20	21
22	23	24	25	26	27	28
29	30	31				

FEBRUARY 2023

S	M	T	W	T	F	S
			1	2	3	4
5	6	7	8	9	10	11
12	13	14	15	16	17	18
19	20	21	22	23	24	25
26	27	28				

MARCH 2023

S	M	T	W	T	F	S
			1	2	3	4
5	6	7	8	9	10	11
12	13	14	15	16	17	18
19	20	21	22	23	24	25
26	27	28	29	30	31	

APRIL 2023

S	M	T	W	T	F	S
						1
2	3	4	5	6	7	8
9	10	11	12	13	14	15
16	17	18	19	20	21	22
$^{23}/_{30}$	24	25	26	27	28	29

MAY 2023

S	M	T	W	T	F	S
	1	2	3	4	5	6
7	8	9	10	11	12	13
14	15	16	17	18	19	20
21	22	23	24	25	26	27
28	29	30	31			

JUNE 2023

S	M	T	W	T	F	S
				1	2	3
4	5	6	7	8	9	10
11	12	13	14	15	16	17
18	19	20	21	22	23	24
25	26	27	28	29	30	

JULY 2023

S	M	T	W	T	F	S
						1
2	3	4	5	6	7	8
9	10	11	12	13	14	15
16	17	18	19	20	21	22
$^{23}/_{30}$	$^{24}/_{31}$	25	26	27	28	29

AUGUST 2023

S	M	T	W	T	F	S
		1	2	3	4	5
6	7	8	9	10	11	12
13	14	15	16	17	18	19
20	21	22	23	24	25	26
27	28	29	30	31		

SEPTEMBER 2023

S	M	T	W	T	F	S
					1	2
3	4	5	6	7	8	9
10	11	12	13	14	15	16
17	18	19	20	21	22	23
24	25	26	27	28	29	30

OCTOBER 2023

S	M	T	W	T	F	S
1	2	3	4	5	6	7
8	9	10	11	12	13	14
15	16	17	18	19	20	21
22	23	24	25	26	27	28
29	30	31				

NOVEMBER 2023

S	M	T	W	T	F	S
			1	2	3	4
5	6	7	8	9	10	11
12	13	14	15	16	17	18
19	20	21	22	23	24	25
26	27	28	29	30		

DECEMBER 2023

S	M	T	W	T	F	S
					1	2
3	4	5	6	7	8	9
10	11	12	13	14	15	16
17	18	19	20	21	22	23
$^{24}/_{31}$	25	26	27	28	29	30

JANUARY 2022

SUNDAY	MONDAY	TUESDAY	WEDNESDAY	THURSDAY	FRIDAY	SATURDAY
26	27	28	29	30	31	1 New Year's Day
2	3 Day after New Year's Day (NZ, SCT)	4	5	6	7	8
9	10	11	12	13	14	15
16	17 Martin Luther King Jr. Day	18	19	20	21	22
23/30	24/31	25	26 Australia Day (AUS)	27	28	29

MONTHLY GOALS

What Worked Last Month

What Could Be Better

New Goals to Focus On

"Change might not be fast and it isn't always easy. But with time and effort, almost any habit can be reshaped."

YOUR HABIT LOOP

To track a new habit, the first step is to **identify your routine**. What is the habit you are focusing on for the month? Next, you will want to **experiment with rewards** over the next few weeks and **isolate your cue**. Once you follow the steps laid out in the introduction, you can **make a plan** to change that habit.

 **Routine**

Experimenting with Rewards

Rewards to test

Write down three words to describe how you are feeling after receiving the reward.

Set an alarm for 15 minutes. Now, are you still craving your old habit?

The identified reward

Isolate your cue

Location

Time

Emotional state

Other people

Preceding action

 **Have a Plan**

What is a new routine that you can implement to change the habit while getting the reward?

Track your habits and watch your progress at a glance by listing some below and coloring in the daily boxes!

HABIT TRACKER

2021/22 DECEMBER/JANUARY

MONDAY
27

TUESDAY
28

WEDNESDAY
29

THURSDAY
30

FRIDAY
31

New Year's Eve

SATURDAY
1

New Year's Day

SUNDAY
2

Day after New Year's Day (NZ, SCT)

DON'T FORGET!

DECEMBER 2021

S	M	T	W	T	F	S
			1	2	3	4
5	6	7	8	9	10	11
12	13	14	15	16	17	18
19	20	21	22	23	24	25
26	27	28	29	30	31	

JANUARY 2022

S	M	T	W	T	F	S
						1
2	3	4	5	6	7	8
9	10	11	12	13	14	15
16	17	18	19	20	21	22
$^{23}/_{30}$	$^{24}/_{31}$	25	26	27	28	29

HABIT REFLECTION

What worked this week?

What didn't? How can you adjust your habit plan or change your experiment for this month?

2022 **JANUARY**

MONDAY
3

TUESDAY
4

WEDNESDAY
5

THURSDAY
6

FRIDAY
7

SATURDAY
8

SUNDAY
9

DON'T FORGET!

JANUARY 2022

S	M	T	W	T	F	S
						1
2	3	4	5	6	7	8
9	10	11	12	13	14	15
16	17	18	19	20	21	22
23/30	24/31	25	26	27	28	29

FEBRUARY 2022

S	M	T	W	T	F	S
		1	2	3	4	5
6	7	8	9	10	11	12
13	14	15	16	17	18	19
20	21	22	23	24	25	26
27	28					

HABIT REFLECTION

What worked this week?

What didn't? How can you adjust your habit plan or change your experiment for this month?

2022 JANUARY

MONDAY
10

TUESDAY
11

WEDNESDAY
12

THURSDAY
13

FRIDAY
14

SATURDAY
15

SUNDAY
16

DON'T FORGET!

JANUARY 2022						
S	M	T	W	T	F	S
						1
2	3	4	5	6	7	8
9	10	11	12	13	14	15
16	17	18	19	20	21	22
23/30	24/31	25	26	27	28	29

FEBRUARY 2022						
S	M	T	W	T	F	S
		1	2	3	4	5
6	7	8	9	10	11	12
13	14	15	16	17	18	19
20	21	22	23	24	25	26
27	28					

HABIT REFLECTION

What worked this week?

What didn't? How can you adjust your habit plan or change your experiment for this month?

2022 **JANUARY**

MONDAY
17

Martin Luther King Jr. Day

TUESDAY
18

WEDNESDAY
19

THURSDAY
20

FRIDAY
21

SATURDAY
22

SUNDAY
23

DON'T FORGET!

JANUARY 2022

S	M	T	W	T	F	S
						1
2	3	4	5	6	7	8
9	10	11	12	13	14	15
16	17	18	19	20	21	22
23/30	24/31	25	26	27	28	29

FEBRUARY 2022

S	M	T	W	T	F	S
		1	2	3	4	5
6	7	8	9	10	11	12
13	14	15	16	17	18	19
20	21	22	23	24	25	26
27	28					

HABIT REFLECTION

What worked this week?

What didn't? How can you adjust your habit plan or change your experiment for this month?

2022 **JANUARY**

MONDAY
24

TUESDAY
25

WEDNESDAY
26

Australia Day (AUS)

THURSDAY
27

FRIDAY
28

SATURDAY
29

SUNDAY
30

DON'T FORGET!

JANUARY 2022

S	M	T	W	T	F	S
						1
2	3	4	5	6	7	8
9	10	11	12	13	14	15
16	17	18	19	20	21	22
23/30	24/31	25	26	27	28	29

FEBRUARY 2022

S	M	T	W	T	F	S
		1	2	3	4	5
6	7	8	9	10	11	12
13	14	15	16	17	18	19
20	21	22	23	24	25	26
27	28					

HABIT REFLECTION

What worked this week?

What didn't? How can you adjust your habit plan or change your experiment for this month?

FEBRUARY 2022

SUNDAY	MONDAY	TUESDAY	WEDNESDAY	THURSDAY	FRIDAY	SATURDAY
30	31	1	2	3	4	5
6	7	8 Chinese New Year	9 Groundhog Day	10	11	12
13 Waitangi Day (NZ)	14 Valentine's Day	15	16	17	18	19 Abraham Lincoln's Birthday
20	21 Presidents' Day	22	23	24	25	26
27	28	1	2	3	4	5

MONTHLY GOALS

What Worked Last Month

What Could Be Better

New Goals to Focus On

"If you believe you can change—if you make it a habit—the change becomes real."

YOUR HABIT LOOP

To track a new habit, the first step is to **identify your routine**. What is the habit you are focusing on for the month? Next, you will want to **experiment with rewards** over the next few weeks and **isolate your cue**. Once you follow the steps laid out in the introduction, you can **make a plan** to change that habit.

 Routine

Experimenting with Rewards

Rewards to test

Write down three words to describe how you are feeling after receiving the reward.

Set an alarm for 15 minutes. Now, are you still craving your old habit?

The identified reward

Isolate your cue

Location

Time

Emotional state

Other people

Preceding action

Have a Plan
What is a new routine that you can implement to change the habit while getting the reward?

Track your habits and watch your progress at a glance by listing some below and coloring in the daily boxes!

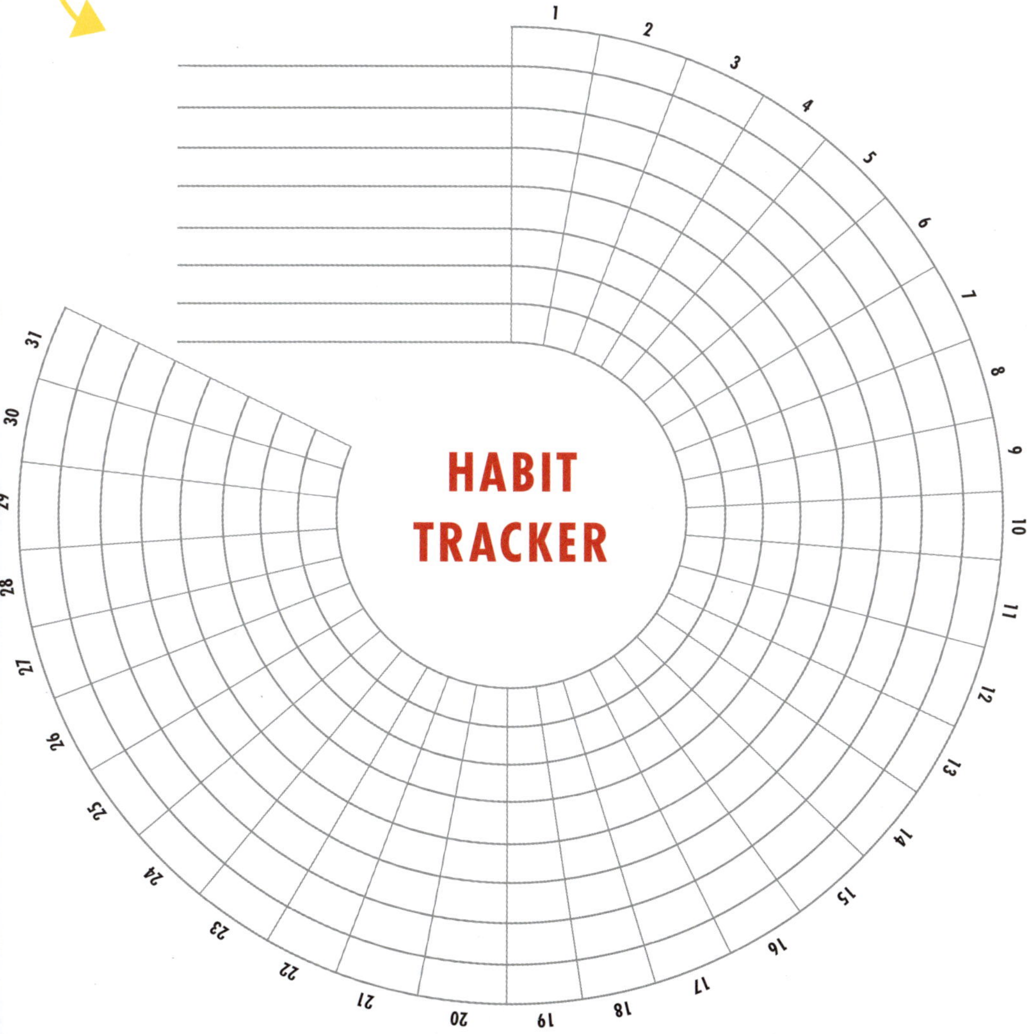

HABIT TRACKER

2022 JANUARY/FEBRUARY

MONDAY
31

TUESDAY
1

Chinese New Year

WEDNESDAY
2

Groundhog Day

THURSDAY
3

FRIDAY
4

SATURDAY
5

SUNDAY
6

Waitangi Day (NZ)

DON'T FORGET!

FEBRUARY 2022

S	M	T	W	T	F	S
		1	2	3	4	5
6	7	8	9	10	11	12
13	14	15	16	17	18	19
20	21	22	23	24	25	26
27	28					

MARCH 2022

S	M	T	W	T	F	S
		1	2	3	4	5
6	7	8	9	10	11	12
13	14	15	16	17	18	19
20	21	22	23	24	25	26
27	28	29	30	31		

HABIT REFLECTION

What worked this week?

What didn't? How can you adjust your habit plan or change your experiment for this month?

2022 FEBRUARY

MONDAY
7

TUESDAY
8

WEDNESDAY
9

THURSDAY
10

FRIDAY
11

SATURDAY
12

SUNDAY
13

Abraham Lincoln's Birthday

DON'T FORGET!

FEBRUARY 2022

S	M	T	W	T	F	S
		1	2	3	4	5
6	7	8	9	10	11	12
13	14	15	16	17	18	19
20	21	22	23	24	25	26
27	28					

MARCH 2022

S	M	T	W	T	F	S
		1	2	3	4	5
6	7	8	9	10	11	12
13	14	15	16	17	18	19
20	21	22	23	24	25	26
27	28	29	30	31		

HABIT REFLECTION

What worked this week?

What didn't? How can you adjust your habit plan or change your experiment for this month?

FEBRUARY 2022

MONDAY
14

Valentine's Day

TUESDAY
15

WEDNESDAY
16

THURSDAY
17

FRIDAY
18

SATURDAY
19

SUNDAY
20

DON'T FORGET!

FEBRUARY 2022

S	M	T	W	T	F	S
		1	2	3	4	5
6	7	8	9	10	11	12
13	14	15	16	17	18	19
20	21	22	23	24	25	26
27	28					

MARCH 2022

S	M	T	W	T	F	S
		1	2	3	4	5
6	7	8	9	10	11	12
13	14	15	16	17	18	19
20	21	22	23	24	25	26
27	28	29	30	31		

HABIT REFLECTION

What worked this week?

What didn't? How can you adjust your habit plan or change your experiment for this month?

2022 FEBRUARY

MONDAY
21

Presidents' Day

TUESDAY
22

WEDNESDAY
23

THURSDAY
24

FRIDAY
25

SATURDAY
26

SUNDAY
27

DON'T FORGET!

FEBRUARY 2022

S	M	T	W	T	F	S
		1	2	3	4	5
6	7	8	9	10	11	12
13	14	15	16	17	18	19
20	21	22	23	24	25	26
27	28					

MARCH 2022

S	M	T	W	T	F	S
		1	2	3	4	5
6	7	8	9	10	11	12
13	14	15	16	17	18	19
20	21	22	23	24	25	26
27	28	29	30	31		

HABIT REFLECTION

What worked this week?

What didn't? How can you adjust your habit plan or change your experiment for this month?

MARCH 2022

SUNDAY	MONDAY	TUESDAY	WEDNESDAY	THURSDAY	FRIDAY	SATURDAY
27	28	1	2	3	4	5
6	7	8	9 Ash Wednesday (Lent begins)	10	11	12
13	14	15 International Women's Day	16	17	18	19
20 Daylight Saving Time begins (USA, CAN)	21 Public Holiday (AUS: ACT, SA, TAS, VIC)	22	23 Purim begins	24 St. Patrick's Day	25	26
27 Spring begins (Northern Hemisphere)	28	29	30	31	1	2 Mothering Sunday (UK)

MONTHLY GOALS

What Worked Last Month

What Could Be Better

New Goals to Focus On

"This is the real power of habit: the insight that your habits are what you choose them to be."

YOUR HABIT LOOP

To track a new habit, the first step is to **identify your routine**. What is the habit you are focusing on for the month? Next, you will want to **experiment with rewards** over the next few weeks and **isolate your cue**. Once you follow the steps laid out in the introduction, you can **make a plan** to change that habit.

 **Routine**

Experimenting with Rewards

Rewards to test

Write down three words to describe how you are feeling after receiving the reward.

Set an alarm for 15 minutes. Now, are you still craving your old habit?

The identified reward

Isolate your cue

Location

Time

Emotional state

Other people

Preceding action

Have a Plan
What is a new routine that you can implement to change the habit while getting the reward?

Track your habits and watch your progress at a glance by listing some below and coloring in the daily boxes!

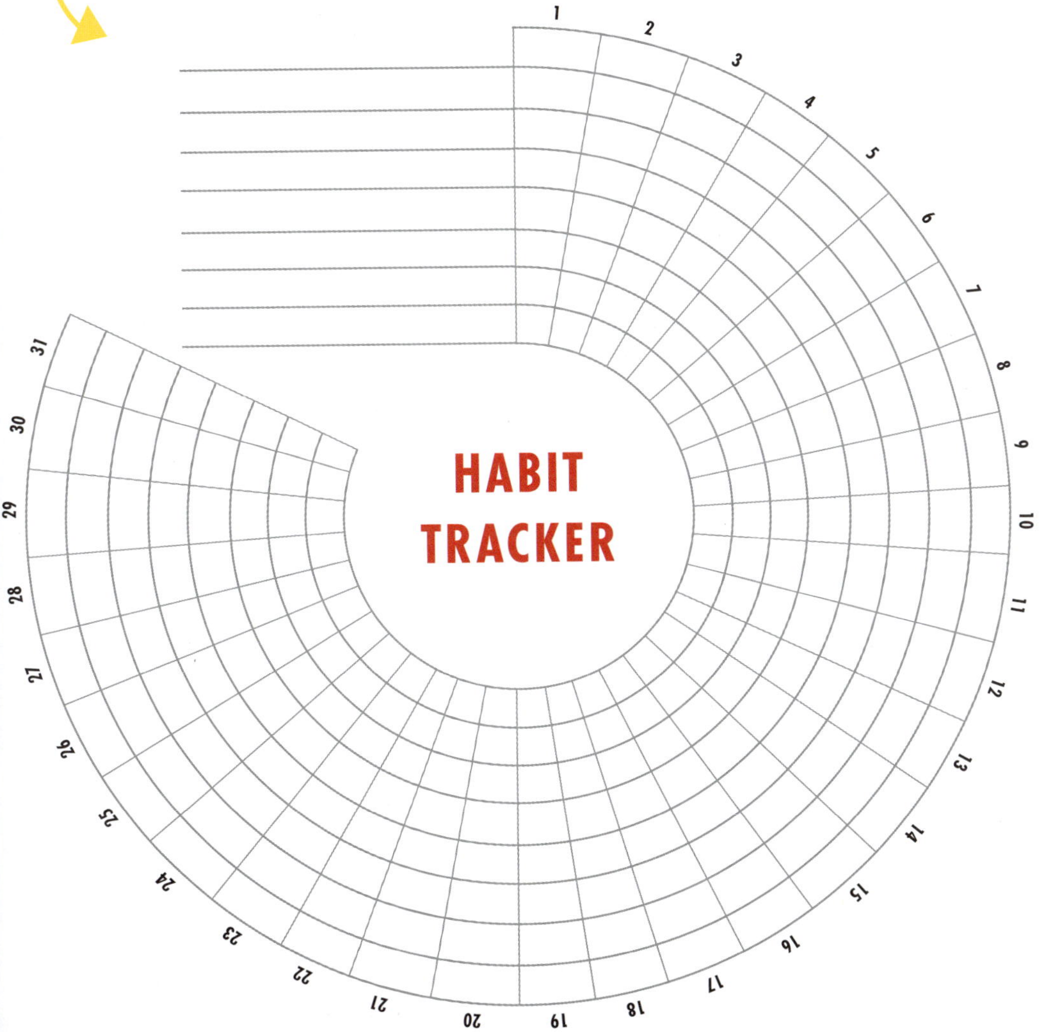

HABIT TRACKER

2022 FEBRUARY/MARCH

MONDAY
28

TUESDAY
1

WEDNESDAY
2

Ash Wednesday (Lent begins)

THURSDAY
3

FRIDAY
4

SATURDAY
5

SUNDAY
6

DON'T FORGET!

MARCH 2022

S	M	T	W	T	F	S
		1	2	3	4	5
6	7	8	9	10	11	12
13	14	15	16	17	18	19
20	21	22	23	24	25	26
27	28	29	30	31		

APRIL 2022

S	M	T	W	T	F	S
					1	2
3	4	5	6	7	8	9
10	11	12	13	14	15	16
17	18	19	20	21	22	23
24	25	26	27	28	29	30

HABIT REFLECTION

What worked this week?

What didn't? How can you adjust your habit plan or change your experiment for this month?

2022 **MARCH**

MONDAY
7

TUESDAY
8

International Women's Day

WEDNESDAY
9

THURSDAY
10

FRIDAY
11

SATURDAY
12

SUNDAY
13

Daylight Saving Time begins (USA, CAN)

DON'T FORGET!

MARCH 2022

S	M	T	W	T	F	S
		1	2	3	4	5
6	7	8	9	10	11	12
13	14	15	16	17	18	19
20	21	22	23	24	25	26
27	28	29	30	31		

APRIL 2022

S	M	T	W	T	F	S
					1	2
3	4	5	6	7	8	9
10	11	12	13	14	15	16
17	18	19	20	21	22	23
24	25	26	27	28	29	30

HABIT REFLECTION

What worked this week?

What didn't? How can you adjust your habit plan or change your experiment for this month?

2022 MARCH

MONDAY
14

Public Holiday (AUS: ACT, SA, TAS, VIC)

TUESDAY
15

WEDNESDAY
16

Purim begins

THURSDAY
17

St. Patrick's Day

FRIDAY
18

SATURDAY
19

SUNDAY
20

Spring begins (Northern Hemisphere)

DON'T FORGET!

MARCH 2022

S	M	T	W	T	F	S
		1	2	3	4	5
6	7	8	9	10	11	12
13	14	15	16	17	18	19
20	21	22	23	24	25	26
27	28	29	30	31		

APRIL 2022

S	M	T	W	T	F	S
					1	2
3	4	5	6	7	8	9
10	11	12	13	14	15	16
17	18	19	20	21	22	23
24	25	26	27	28	29	30

HABIT REFLECTION

What worked this week?

What didn't? How can you adjust your habit plan or change your experiment for this month?

2022 **MARCH**

MONDAY
21

TUESDAY
22

WEDNESDAY
23

THURSDAY
24

FRIDAY
25

SATURDAY
26

SUNDAY
27

Mothering Sunday (UK)

DON'T FORGET!

MARCH 2022								**APRIL 2022**						
S	M	T	W	T	F	S		S	M	T	W	T	F	S
		1	2	3	4	5							1	2
6	7	8	9	10	11	12		3	4	5	6	7	8	9
13	14	15	16	17	18	19		10	11	12	13	14	15	16
20	21	22	23	24	25	26		17	18	19	20	21	22	23
27	28	29	30	31				24	25	26	27	28	29	30

HABIT REFLECTION

What worked this week?

What didn't? How can you adjust your habit plan or change your experiment for this month?

2022 MARCH/APRIL

MONDAY
28

TUESDAY
29

WEDNESDAY
30

THURSDAY
31

FRIDAY
1

April Fools' Day

SATURDAY
2

SUNDAY
3

Ramadan begins

DON'T FORGET!

MARCH 2022

S	M	T	W	T	F	S
		1	2	3	4	5
6	7	8	9	10	11	12
13	14	15	16	17	18	19
20	21	22	23	24	25	26
27	28	29	30	31		

APRIL 2022

S	M	T	W	T	F	S
					1	2
3	4	5	6	7	8	9
10	11	12	13	14	15	16
17	18	19	20	21	22	23
24	25	26	27	28	29	30

HABIT REFLECTION

What worked this week?

What didn't? How can you adjust your habit plan or change your experiment for this month?

APRIL 2022

SUNDAY	MONDAY	TUESDAY	WEDNESDAY	THURSDAY	FRIDAY	SATURDAY
27	28	29	30	31	1 April Fools' Day	2 Ramadan begins
3	4	5	6	7	8	9
10 Palm Sunday	11	12	13	14	15	16
17	18 Tax Day; Easter Monday (AUS, CAN, NZ, UK except SCT)	19	20	21	22 Good Friday; Passover begins	23
24 Easter	25 Anzac Day (AUS, NZ)	26	27	28	29 Earth Day	30
				Workers' Memorial Day (UK)		

MONTHLY GOALS

What Worked Last Month

What Could Be Better

New Goals to Focus On

"The habits that matter most are the ones that, when they start to shift, dislodge and remake other patterns."

YOUR HABIT LOOP

To track a new habit, the first step is to **identify your routine**. What is the habit you are focusing on for the month? Next, you will want to **experiment with rewards** over the next few weeks and **isolate your cue**. Once you follow the steps laid out in the introduction, you can **make a plan** to change that habit.

 Routine

Experimenting with Rewards

Rewards to test

Write down three words to describe how you are feeling after receiving the reward.

Set an alarm for 15 minutes. Now, are you still craving your old habit?

The identified reward

Isolate your cue

Location

Time

Emotional state

Other people

Preceding action

Have a Plan
What is a new routine that you can implement to change the habit while getting the reward?

Track your habits and watch your progress at a glance by listing some below and coloring in the daily boxes!

HABIT TRACKER

2022 APRIL

MONDAY
4

TUESDAY
5

WEDNESDAY
6

THURSDAY
7

FRIDAY
8

SATURDAY
9

SUNDAY
10

Palm Sunday

DON'T FORGET!

APRIL 2022

S	M	T	W	T	F	S
					1	2
3	4	5	6	7	8	9
10	11	12	13	14	15	16
17	18	19	20	21	22	23
24	25	26	27	28	29	30

MAY 2022

S	M	T	W	T	F	S
1	2	3	4	5	6	7
8	9	10	11	12	13	14
15	16	17	18	19	20	21
22	23	24	25	26	27	28
29	30	31				

HABIT REFLECTION

What worked this week?

What didn't? How can you adjust your habit plan or change your experiment for this month?

2022 **APRIL**

MONDAY
11

TUESDAY
12

WEDNESDAY
13

THURSDAY
14

FRIDAY
15

Good Friday; Passover begins

SATURDAY
16

SUNDAY
17

Easter

DON'T FORGET!

APRIL 2022

S	M	T	W	T	F	S
					1	2
3	4	5	6	7	8	9
10	11	12	13	14	15	16
17	18	19	20	21	22	23
24	25	26	27	28	29	30

MAY 2022

S	M	T	W	T	F	S
1	2	3	4	5	6	7
8	9	10	11	12	13	14
15	16	17	18	19	20	21
22	23	24	25	26	27	28
29	30	31				

HABIT REFLECTION

What worked this week?

What didn't? How can you adjust your habit plan or change your experiment for this month?

2022 APRIL

MONDAY
18

Tax Day; Easter Monday (AUS, CAN, NZ, UK except SCT)

TUESDAY
19

WEDNESDAY
20

THURSDAY
21

FRIDAY 22

Earth Day

SATURDAY 23

SUNDAY 24

DON'T FORGET!

APRIL 2022

S	M	T	W	T	F	S
					1	2
3	4	5	6	7	8	9
10	11	12	13	14	15	16
17	18	19	20	21	22	23
24	25	26	27	28	29	30

MAY 2022

S	M	T	W	T	F	S
1	2	3	4	5	6	7
8	9	10	11	12	13	14
15	16	17	18	19	20	21
22	23	24	25	26	27	28
29	30	31				

HABIT REFLECTION

What worked this week?

What didn't? How can you adjust your habit plan or change your experiment for this month?

2022 APRIL/MAY

MONDAY
25

Anzac Day (AUS, NZ)

TUESDAY
26

WEDNESDAY
27

THURSDAY
28

Workers' Memorial Day (UK)

FRIDAY
29

SATURDAY
30

SUNDAY
1

DON'T FORGET!

APRIL 2022

S	M	T	W	T	F	S
					1	2
3	4	5	6	7	8	9
10	11	12	13	14	15	16
17	18	19	20	21	22	23
24	25	26	27	28	29	30

MAY 2022

S	M	T	W	T	F	S
1	2	3	4	5	6	7
8	9	10	11	12	13	14
15	16	17	18	19	20	21
22	23	24	25	26	27	28
29	30	31				

HABIT REFLECTION

What worked this week?

What didn't? How can you adjust your habit plan or change your experiment for this month?

MAY 2022

SUNDAY	MONDAY	TUESDAY	WEDNESDAY	THURSDAY	FRIDAY	SATURDAY
1	2	3	4	5	6	7
8 Mother's Day (USA, AUS, CAN, NZ)	9 Eid al-Fitr begins	10	11	12	13	14
15	16	17	18	19	20	21 Armed Forces Day
22	23	24	25	26	27	28
29	30 Victoria Day (CAN)	31	1	2	3	4
	Memorial Day (USA); Spring Bank Holiday (UK)					

Cinco de Mayo — 5

MONTHLY GOALS

What Worked Last Month

What Could Be Better

New Goals to Focus On

"We can choose our habits, once we know how."

YOUR HABIT LOOP

To track a new habit, the first step is to **identify your routine**. What is the habit you are focusing on for the month? Next, you will want to **experiment with rewards** over the next few weeks and **isolate your cue**. Once you follow the steps laid out in the introduction, you can **make a plan** to change that habit.

 **Routine**

Experimenting with Rewards

Rewards to test

Write down three words to describe how you are feeling after receiving the reward.

Set an alarm for 15 minutes. Now, are you still craving your old habit?

The identified reward

Isolate your cue

Location

Time

Emotional state

Other people

Preceding action

Have a Plan
What is a new routine that you can implement to change the habit while getting the reward?

Track your habits and watch your progress at a glance by listing some below and coloring in the daily boxes!

HABIT TRACKER

2022 **MAY**

MONDAY
2

Eid al-Fitr begins

TUESDAY
3

WEDNESDAY
4

THURSDAY
5

Cinco de Mayo

FRIDAY
6

SATURDAY
7

SUNDAY
8

Mother's Day (USA, AUS, CAN, NZ)

DON'T FORGET!

MAY 2022

S	M	T	W	T	F	S
1	2	3	4	5	6	7
8	9	10	11	12	13	14
15	16	17	18	19	20	21
22	23	24	25	26	27	28
29	30	31				

JUNE 2022

S	M	T	W	T	F	S
			1	2	3	4
5	6	7	8	9	10	11
12	13	14	15	16	17	18
19	20	21	22	23	24	25
26	27	28	29	30		

HABIT REFLECTION

What worked this week?

What didn't? How can you adjust your habit plan or change your experiment for this month?

2022 **MAY**

MONDAY
9

TUESDAY
10

WEDNESDAY
11

THURSDAY
12

FRIDAY
13

SATURDAY
14

SUNDAY
15

DON'T FORGET!

MAY 2022						
S	M	T	W	T	F	S
1	2	3	4	5	6	7
8	9	10	11	12	13	14
15	16	17	18	19	20	21
22	23	24	25	26	27	28
29	30	31				

JUNE 2022						
S	M	T	W	T	F	S
			1	2	3	4
5	6	7	8	9	10	11
12	13	14	15	16	17	18
19	20	21	22	23	24	25
26	27	28	29	30		

HABIT REFLECTION

What worked this week?

What didn't? How can you adjust your habit plan or change your experiment for this month?

2022 **MAY**

MONDAY
16

TUESDAY
17

WEDNESDAY
18

THURSDAY
19

FRIDAY
20

SATURDAY
21

SUNDAY
22

Armed Forces Day

DON'T FORGET!

MAY 2022

S	M	T	W	T	F	S
1	2	3	4	5	6	7
8	9	10	11	12	13	14
15	16	17	18	19	20	21
22	23	24	25	26	27	28
29	30	31				

JUNE 2022

S	M	T	W	T	F	S
			1	2	3	4
5	6	7	8	9	10	11
12	13	14	15	16	17	18
19	20	21	22	23	24	25
26	27	28	29	30		

HABIT REFLECTION

What worked this week?

What didn't? How can you adjust your habit plan or change your experiment for this month?

2022 **MAY**

MONDAY
23

Victoria Day (CAN)

TUESDAY
24

WEDNESDAY
25

THURSDAY
26

FRIDAY
27

SATURDAY
28

SUNDAY
29

DON'T FORGET!

MAY 2022

S	M	T	W	T	F	S
1	2	3	4	5	6	7
8	9	10	11	12	13	14
15	16	17	18	19	20	21
22	23	24	25	26	27	28
29	30	31				

JUNE 2022

S	M	T	W	T	F	S
			1	2	3	4
5	6	7	8	9	10	11
12	13	14	15	16	17	18
19	20	21	22	23	24	25
26	27	28	29	30		

HABIT REFLECTION

What worked this week?

What didn't? How can you adjust your habit plan or change your experiment for this month?

JUNE 2022

SUNDAY	MONDAY	TUESDAY	WEDNESDAY	THURSDAY	FRIDAY	SATURDAY
29	30	31	1	2	3	4
5	6	7	8	9	10	11 Shavuot begins
12	13	14	15	16	17	18
19 Father's Day (USA, CAN, UK); Juneteenth	20	21 Flag Day	22	23	24	25
26	27	28 Summer begins (Northern Hemisphere)	29	30	1	2

MONTHLY GOALS

What Worked Last Month

What Could Be Better

New Goals to Focus On

"Habits are powerful, but delicate. They can emerge outside our consciousness, or can be deliberately designed."

YOUR HABIT LOOP

To track a new habit, the first step is to **identify your routine**. What is the habit you are focusing on for the month? Next, you will want to **experiment with rewards** over the next few weeks and **isolate your cue**. Once you follow the steps laid out in the introduction, you can **make a plan** to change that habit.

 **Routine**

Experimenting with Rewards

Rewards to test

Write down three words to describe how you are feeling after receiving the reward.

Set an alarm for 15 minutes. Now, are you still craving your old habit?

The identified reward

Isolate your cue

Location

Time

Emotional state

Other people

Preceding action

Have a Plan
What is a new routine that you can implement to change the habit while getting the reward?

Track your habits and watch your progress at a glance by listing some below and coloring in the daily boxes!

HABIT TRACKER

2022 MAY/JUNE

MONDAY
30

Memorial Day (USA); Spring Bank Holiday (UK)

TUESDAY
31

WEDNESDAY
1

THURSDAY
2

FRIDAY
3

SATURDAY
4

Shavuot begins

SUNDAY
5

DON'T FORGET!

JUNE 2022

S	M	T	W	T	F	S
			1	2	3	4
5	6	7	8	9	10	11
12	13	14	15	16	17	18
19	20	21	22	23	24	25
26	27	28	29	30		

JULY 2022

S	M	T	W	T	F	S
					1	2
3	4	5	6	7	8	9
10	11	12	13	14	15	16
17	18	19	20	21	22	23
24/31	25	26	27	28	29	30

HABIT REFLECTION

What worked this week?

What didn't? How can you adjust your habit plan or change your experiment for this month?

2022 **JUNE**

MONDAY
6

TUESDAY
7

WEDNESDAY
8

THURSDAY
9

FRIDAY
10

SATURDAY
11

SUNDAY
12

DON'T FOREGET!

JUNE 2022						
S	M	T	W	T	F	S
			1	2	3	4
5	6	7	8	9	10	11
12	13	14	15	16	17	18
19	20	21	22	23	24	25
26	27	28	29	30		

JULY 2022						
S	M	T	W	T	F	S
					1	2
3	4	5	6	7	8	9
10	11	12	13	14	15	16
17	18	19	20	21	22	23
$^{24}/_{31}$	25	26	27	28	29	30

HABIT REFLECTION

What worked this week?

What didn't? How can you adjust your habit plan or change your experiment for this month?

2022 JUNE

MONDAY
13

TUESDAY
14

Flag Day

WEDNESDAY
15

THURSDAY
16

FRIDAY
17

SATURDAY
18

SUNDAY
19

Father's Day (USA, CAN, UK); Juneteenth

DON'T FORGET!

JUNE 2022						
S	M	T	W	T	F	S
			1	2	3	4
5	6	7	8	9	10	11
12	13	14	15	16	17	18
19	20	21	22	23	24	25
26	27	28	29	30		

JULY 2022						
S	M	T	W	T	F	S
					1	2
3	4	5	6	7	8	9
10	11	12	13	14	15	16
17	18	19	20	21	22	23
24/31	25	26	27	28	29	30

HABIT REFLECTION

What worked this week?

What didn't? How can you adjust your habit plan or change your experiment for this month?

2022 JUNE

MONDAY
20

TUESDAY
21

Summer begins (Northern Hemisphere)

WEDNESDAY
22

THURSDAY
23

FRIDAY
24

SATURDAY
25

SUNDAY
26

DON'T FORGET!

JUNE 2022

S	M	T	W	T	F	S
			1	2	3	4
5	6	7	8	9	10	11
12	13	14	15	16	17	18
19	20	21	22	23	24	25
26	27	28	29	30		

JULY 2022

S	M	T	W	T	F	S
					1	2
3	4	5	6	7	8	9
10	11	12	13	14	15	16
17	18	19	20	21	22	23
24/31	25	26	27	28	29	30

HABIT REFLECTION

What worked this week?

What didn't? How can you adjust your habit plan or change your experiment for this month?

2022 JUNE/JULY

MONDAY
27

TUESDAY
28

WEDNESDAY
29

THURSDAY
30

FRIDAY
1

Canada Day (CAN)

SATURDAY
2

SUNDAY
3

DON'T FORGET!

JUNE 2022

S	M	T	W	T	F	S
			1	2	3	4
5	6	7	8	9	10	11
12	13	14	15	16	17	18
19	20	21	22	23	24	25
26	27	28	29	30		

JULY 2022

S	M	T	W	T	F	S
					1	2
3	4	5	6	7	8	9
10	11	12	13	14	15	16
17	18	19	20	21	22	23
$^{24}/_{31}$	25	26	27	28	29	30

HABIT REFLECTION

What worked this week?

What didn't? How can you adjust your habit plan or change your experiment for this month?

JULY 2022

SUNDAY	MONDAY	TUESDAY	WEDNESDAY	THURSDAY	FRIDAY	SATURDAY
26	27	28	29	30	1 Canada Day (CAN)	2
3	4 Independence Day	5	6	7	8	9
10	11	12 Orangemen's Day—Battle of the Boyne (NIR)	13	14	15	16 Eid al-Adha begins
17	18	19	20	21	22	23
24/31	25	26	27	28	29	30

MONTHLY GOALS

What Worked Last Month

What Could Be Better

New Goals to Focus On

"Transforming a habit isn't necessarily easy or quick. It isn't always simple. But it is possible."

YOUR HABIT LOOP

To track a new habit, the first step is to **identify your routine**. What is the habit you are focusing on for the month? Next, you will want to **experiment with rewards** over the next few weeks and **isolate your cue**. Once you follow the steps laid out in the introduction, you can **make a plan** to change that habit.

 Routine

Experimenting with Rewards

Rewards to test

Write down three words to describe how you are feeling after receiving the reward.

Set an alarm for 15 minutes. Now, are you still craving your old habit?

The identified reward

Isolate your cue

Location

Time

Emotional state

Other people

Preceding action

Have a Plan
What is a new routine that you can implement to change the habit while getting the reward?

Track your habits and watch your progress at a glance by listing some below and coloring in the daily boxes!

HABIT TRACKER

2022 **JULY**

MONDAY
4

Independence Day

TUESDAY
5

WEDNESDAY
6

THURSDAY
7

FRIDAY
8

SATURDAY
9

Eid al-Adha begins

SUNDAY
10

DON'T FORGET!

JULY 2022

S	M	T	W	T	F	S
					1	2
3	4	5	6	7	8	9
10	11	12	13	14	15	16
17	18	19	20	21	22	23
24/31	25	26	27	28	29	30

AUGUST 2022

S	M	T	W	T	F	S
	1	2	3	4	5	6
7	8	9	10	11	12	13
14	15	16	17	18	19	20
21	22	23	24	25	26	27
28	29	30	31			

HABIT REFLECTION

What worked this week?

What didn't? How can you adjust your habit plan or change your experiment for this month?

2022 **JULY**

MONDAY
11

TUESDAY
12

Orangemen's Day—Battle of the Boyne (NIR)

WEDNESDAY
13

THURSDAY
14

FRIDAY
15

SATURDAY
16

SUNDAY
17

DON'T FORGET!

	JULY 2022							AUGUST 2022					
S	M	T	W	T	F	S	S	M	T	W	T	F	S
					1	2		1	2	3	4	5	6
3	4	5	6	7	8	9	7	8	9	10	11	12	13
10	11	12	13	14	15	16	14	15	16	17	18	19	20
17	18	19	20	21	22	23	21	22	23	24	25	26	27
24/31	25	26	27	28	29	30	28	29	30	31			

HABIT REFLECTION

What worked this week?

What didn't? How can you adjust your habit plan or change your experiment for this month?

2022 **JULY**

MONDAY
18

TUESDAY
19

WEDNESDAY
20

THURSDAY
21

FRIDAY
22

SATURDAY
23

SUNDAY
24

DON'T FORGET!

JULY 2022

S	M	T	W	T	F	S
					1	2
3	4	5	6	7	8	9
10	11	12	13	14	15	16
17	18	19	20	21	22	23
²⁴/₃₁	25	26	27	28	29	30

AUGUST 2022

S	M	T	W	T	F	S
	1	2	3	4	5	6
7	8	9	10	11	12	13
14	15	16	17	18	19	20
21	22	23	24	25	26	27
28	29	30	31			

HABIT REFLECTION

What worked this week?

What didn't? How can you adjust your habit plan or change your experiment for this month?

2022   **JULY**

MONDAY
25

TUESDAY
26

WEDNESDAY
27

THURSDAY
28

FRIDAY
29

SATURDAY
30

SUNDAY
31

DON'T FORGET!

JULY 2022

S	M	T	W	T	F	S
					1	2
3	4	5	6	7	8	9
10	11	12	13	14	15	16
17	18	19	20	21	22	23
$^{24}/_{31}$	25	26	27	28	29	30

AUGUST 2022

S	M	T	W	T	F	S
	1	2	3	4	5	6
7	8	9	10	11	12	13
14	15	16	17	18	19	20
21	22	23	24	25	26	27
28	29	30	31			

HABIT REFLECTION

What worked this week?

What didn't? How can you adjust your habit plan or change your experiment for this month?

AUGUST 2022

SUNDAY	MONDAY	TUESDAY	WEDNESDAY	THURSDAY	FRIDAY	SATURDAY
31	1	2	3	4	5	6
7	8 *Summer Bank Holiday (SCT)*	9	10	11	12	13
14	15	16	17	18	19	20
21	22	23	24	25	26	27
28	29 *Summer Bank Holiday (UK except SCT)*	30	31	1	2	3

MONTHLY GOALS

What Worked Last Month

What Could Be Better

New Goals to Focus On

"The Golden Rule of habit change: You can't extinguish a bad habit, you can only change it."

YOUR HABIT LOOP

To track a new habit, the first step is to **identify your routine**. What is the habit you are focusing on for the month? Next, you will want to **experiment with rewards** over the next few weeks and **isolate your cue**. Once you follow the steps laid out in the introduction, you can **make a plan** to change that habit.

 Routine

Experimenting with Rewards

Rewards to test

Write down three words to describe how you are feeling after receiving the reward.

Set an alarm for 15 minutes. Now, are you still craving your old habit?

The identified reward

Isolate your cue

Location

Time

Emotional state

Other people

Preceding action

Have a Plan
What is a new routine that you can implement to change the habit while getting the reward?

Track your habits and watch your progress at a glance by listing some below and coloring in the daily boxes!

HABIT TRACKER

2022 AUGUST

MONDAY
1

Summer Bank Holiday (SCT)

TUESDAY
2

WEDNESDAY
3

THURSDAY
4

FRIDAY
5

SATURDAY
6

SUNDAY
7

DON'T FORGET!

AUGUST 2022						
S	M	T	W	T	F	S
	1	2	3	4	5	6
7	8	9	10	11	12	13
14	15	16	17	18	19	20
21	22	23	24	25	26	27
28	29	30	31			

SEPTEMBER 2022						
S	M	T	W	T	F	S
				1	2	3
4	5	6	7	8	9	10
11	12	13	14	15	16	17
18	19	20	21	22	23	24
25	26	27	28	29	30	

HABIT REFLECTION

What worked this week?

What didn't? How can you adjust your habit plan or change your experiment for this month?

2022 **AUGUST**

MONDAY
8

TUESDAY
9

WEDNESDAY
10

THURSDAY
11

FRIDAY
12

SATURDAY
13

SUNDAY
14

DON'T FORGET!

AUGUST 2022

S	M	T	W	T	F	S
	1	2	3	4	5	6
7	8	9	10	11	12	13
14	15	16	17	18	19	20
21	22	23	24	25	26	27
28	29	30	31			

SEPTEMBER 2022

S	M	T	W	T	F	S
				1	2	3
4	5	6	7	8	9	10
11	12	13	14	15	16	17
18	19	20	21	22	23	24
25	26	27	28	29	30	

HABIT REFLECTION

What worked this week?

What didn't? How can you adjust your habit plan or change your experiment for this month?

2022 AUGUST

MONDAY
15

TUESDAY
16

WEDNESDAY
17

THURSDAY
18

FRIDAY
19

SATURDAY
20

SUNDAY
21

DON'T FORGET!

AUGUST 2022							**SEPTEMBER 2022**						
S	M	T	W	T	F	S	S	M	T	W	T	F	S
	1	2	3	4	5	6					1	2	3
7	8	9	10	11	12	13	4	5	6	7	8	9	10
14	15	16	17	18	19	20	11	12	13	14	15	16	17
21	22	23	24	25	26	27	18	19	20	21	22	23	24
28	29	30	31				25	26	27	28	29	30	

HABIT REFLECTION

What worked this week?

What didn't? How can you adjust your habit plan or change your experiment for this month?

2022 AUGUST

MONDAY
22

TUESDAY
23

WEDNESDAY
24

THURSDAY
25

FRIDAY
26

SATURDAY
27

SUNDAY
28

DON'T FORGET!

AUGUST 2022

S	M	T	W	T	F	S
	1	2	3	4	5	6
7	8	9	10	11	12	13
14	15	16	17	18	19	20
21	22	23	24	25	26	27
28	29	30	31			

SEPTEMBER 2022

S	M	T	W	T	F	S
				1	2	3
4	5	6	7	8	9	10
11	12	13	14	15	16	17
18	19	20	21	22	23	24
25	26	27	28	29	30	

HABIT REFLECTION

What worked this week?

What didn't? How can you adjust your habit plan or change your experiment for this month?

SEPTEMBER 2022

SUNDAY	MONDAY	TUESDAY	WEDNESDAY	THURSDAY	FRIDAY	SATURDAY
28	29	30	31	1	2	3
4	5	6	7	8	9	10
11 Father's Day (AUS, NZ)	12 Labor Day (USA, CAN)	13	14	15	16	17
18 Patriot Day	19	20	21	22	23 Autumn begins (Northern Hemisphere)	24
25 Rosh Hashanah begins	26	27	28	29	30	1

MONTHLY GOALS

What Worked Last Month

What Could Be Better

New Goals to Focus On

"This is how willpower becomes a habit: by choosing a certain behavior ahead of time, and then following that routine when an inflection point arrives."

YOUR HABIT LOOP

To track a new habit, the first step is to **identify your routine**. What is the habit you are focusing on for the month? Next, you will want to **experiment with rewards** over the next few weeks and **isolate your cue**. Once you follow the steps laid out in the introduction, you can **make a plan** to change that habit.

 Routine

Experimenting with Rewards

Rewards to test

Write down three words to describe how you are feeling after receiving the reward.

Set an alarm for 15 minutes. Now, are you still craving your old habit?

The identified reward

Isolate your cue

Location

Time

Emotional state

Other people

Preceding action

Have a Plan
What is a new routine that you can implement to change the habit while getting the reward?

Track your habits and watch your progress at a glance by listing some below and coloring in the daily boxes!

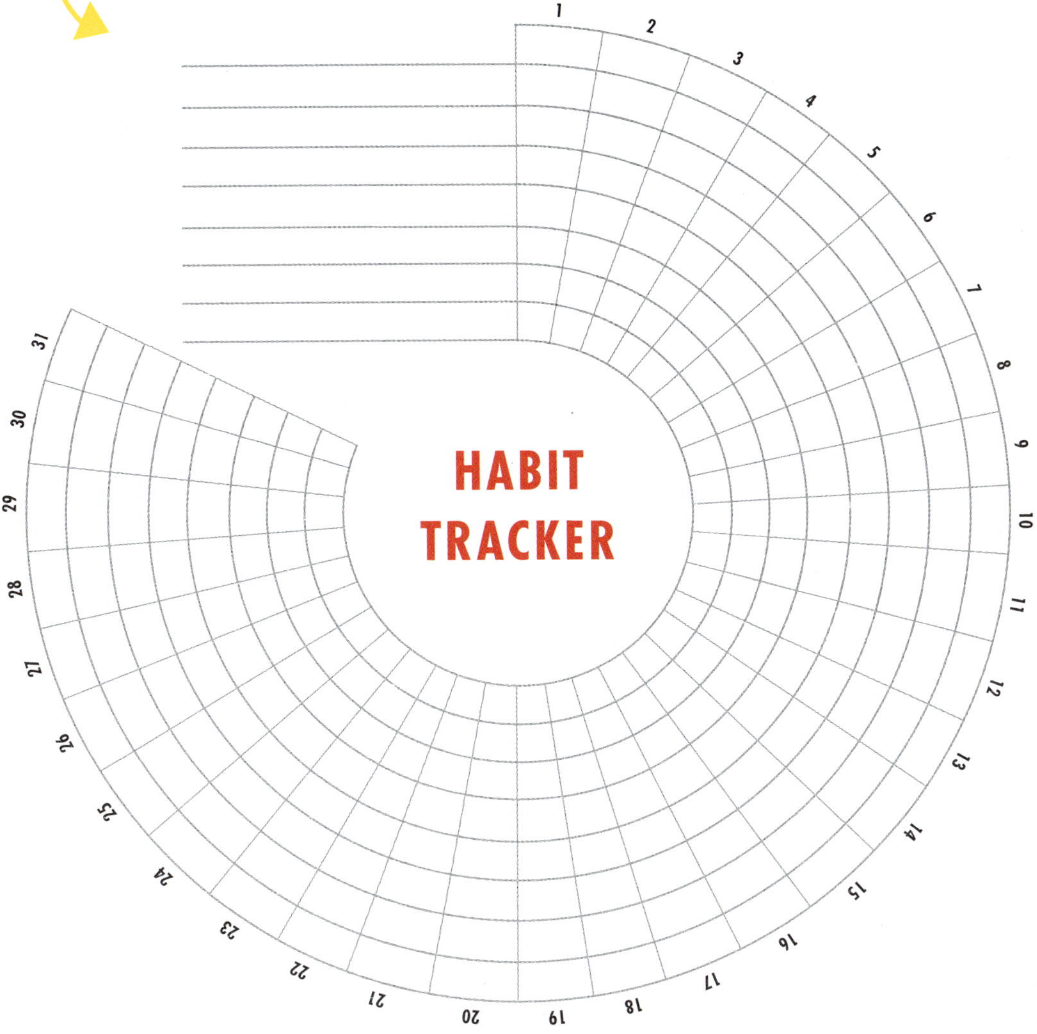

HABIT TRACKER

2022 AUGUST/SEPTEMBER

MONDAY
29

Summer Bank Holiday (UK except SCT)

TUESDAY
30

WEDNESDAY
31

THURSDAY
1

FRIDAY
2

SATURDAY
3

SUNDAY
4

Father's Day (AUS, NZ)

DON'T FORGET!

SEPTEMBER 2022

S	M	T	W	T	F	S
				1	2	3
4	5	6	7	8	9	10
11	12	13	14	15	16	17
18	19	20	21	22	23	24
25	26	27	28	29	30	

OCTOBER 2022

S	M	T	W	T	F	S
						1
2	3	4	5	6	7	8
9	10	11	12	13	14	15
16	17	18	19	20	21	22
23/30	24/31	25	26	27	28	29

HABIT REFLECTION

What worked this week?

What didn't? How can you adjust your habit plan or change your experiment for this month?

2022 SEPTEMBER

MONDAY
5

Labor Day (USA, CAN)

TUESDAY
6

WEDNESDAY
7

THURSDAY
8

FRIDAY
9

SATURDAY
10

SUNDAY
11

Patriot Day

DON'T FORGET!

SEPTEMBER 2022

S	M	T	W	T	F	S
				1	2	3
4	5	6	7	8	9	10
11	12	13	14	15	16	17
18	19	20	21	22	23	24
25	26	27	28	29	30	

OCTOBER 2022

S	M	T	W	T	F	S
						1
2	3	4	5	6	7	8
9	10	11	12	13	14	15
16	17	18	19	20	21	22
$^{23}/_{30}$	$^{24}/_{31}$	25	26	27	28	29

HABIT REFLECTION

What worked this week?

What didn't? How can you adjust your habit plan or change your experiment for this month?

2022 **SEPTEMBER**

MONDAY
12

TUESDAY
13

WEDNESDAY
14

THURSDAY
15

FRIDAY
16

SATURDAY
17

SUNDAY
18

DON'T FORGET!

SEPTEMBER 2022						
S	M	T	W	T	F	S
				1	2	3
4	5	6	7	8	9	10
11	12	13	14	15	16	17
18	19	20	21	22	23	24
25	26	27	28	29	30	

OCTOBER 2022						
S	M	T	W	T	F	S
						1
2	3	4	5	6	7	8
9	10	11	12	13	14	15
16	17	18	19	20	21	22
23/30	24/31	25	26	27	28	29

HABIT REFLECTION

What worked this week?

What didn't? How can you adjust your habit plan or change your experiment for this month?

2022 SEPTEMBER

MONDAY
19

TUESDAY
20

WEDNESDAY
21

THURSDAY
22

FRIDAY
23

Autumn begins (Northern Hemisphere)

SATURDAY
24

SUNDAY
25

Rosh Hashanah begins

DON'T FORGET!

SEPTEMBER 2022						
S	M	T	W	T	F	S
				1	2	3
4	5	6	7	8	9	10
11	12	13	14	15	16	17
18	19	20	21	22	23	24
25	26	27	28	29	30	

OCTOBER 2022						
S	M	T	W	T	F	S
						1
2	3	4	5	6	7	8
9	10	11	12	13	14	15
16	17	18	19	20	21	22
$23/30$	$24/31$	25	26	27	28	29

HABIT REFLECTION

What worked this week?

What didn't? How can you adjust your habit plan or change your experiment for this month?

2022 **SEPTEMBER/OCTOBER**

MONDAY
26

TUESDAY
27

WEDNESDAY
28

THURSDAY
29

FRIDAY
30

SATURDAY
1

SUNDAY
2

DON'T FORGET!

SEPTEMBER 2022

S	M	T	W	T	F	S
				1	2	3
4	5	6	7	8	9	10
11	12	13	14	15	16	17
18	19	20	21	22	23	24
25	26	27	28	29	30	

OCTOBER 2022

S	M	T	W	T	F	S
						1
2	3	4	5	6	7	8
9	10	11	12	13	14	15
16	17	18	19	20	21	22
$^{23}/_{30}$	$^{24}/_{31}$	25	26	27	28	29

HABIT REFLECTION

What worked this week?

What didn't? How can you adjust your habit plan or change your experiment for this month?

OCTOBER 2022

SUNDAY	MONDAY	TUESDAY	WEDNESDAY	THURSDAY	FRIDAY	SATURDAY
25	26	27	28	29	30	1
2	3	4	5	6	7	8
9	10	11 Yom Kippur begins	12	13	14	15
16 Sukkot begins	17 Columbus Day (USA); Thanksgiving Day (CAN)	18	19	20	21	22
23/30	24/31 Diwali begins (24th); Halloween (31st)	25	26	27	28	29

MONTHLY GOALS

What Worked Last Month

What Could Be Better

New Goals to Focus On

"As people strengthened their willpower muscles in one part of their lives...that strength spilled over... Once willpower became stronger, it touched everything."

YOUR HABIT LOOP

To track a new habit, the first step is to **identify your routine**. What is the habit you are focusing on for the month? Next, you will want to **experiment with rewards** over the next few weeks and **isolate your cue**. Once you follow the steps laid out in the introduction, you can **make a plan** to change that habit.

 Routine

Experimenting with Rewards

Rewards to test

Write down three words to describe how you are feeling after receiving the reward.

Set an alarm for 15 minutes. Now, are you still craving your old habit?

The identified reward

Isolate your cue

Location

Time

Emotional state

Other people

Preceding action

Have a Plan
What is a new routine that you can implement to change the habit while getting the reward?

Track your habits and watch your progress at a glance by listing some below and coloring in the daily boxes!

HABIT TRACKER

2022 OCTOBER

MONDAY
3

TUESDAY
4

Yom Kippur begins

WEDNESDAY
5

THURSDAY
6

FRIDAY
7

SATURDAY
8

SUNDAY
9

Sukkot begins

DON'T FORGET!

OCTOBER 2022

S	M	T	W	T	F	S
						1
2	3	4	5	6	7	8
9	10	11	12	13	14	15
16	17	18	19	20	21	22
23/30	24/31	25	26	27	28	29

NOVEMBER 2022

S	M	T	W	T	F	S
		1	2	3	4	5
6	7	8	9	10	11	12
13	14	15	16	17	18	19
20	21	22	23	24	25	26
27	28	29	30			

HABIT REFLECTION

What worked this week?

What didn't? How can you adjust your habit plan or change your experiment for this month?

2022 **OCTOBER**

MONDAY
10

Columbus Day (USA); Thanksgiving Day (CAN)

TUESDAY
11

WEDNESDAY
12

THURSDAY
13

FRIDAY
14

SATURDAY
15

SUNDAY
16

DON'T FORGET!

OCTOBER 2022

S	M	T	W	T	F	S
						1
2	3	4	5	6	7	8
9	10	11	12	13	14	15
16	17	18	19	20	21	22
23/30	24/31	25	26	27	28	29

NOVEMBER 2022

S	M	T	W	T	F	S
		1	2	3	4	5
6	7	8	9	10	11	12
13	14	15	16	17	18	19
20	21	22	23	24	25	26
27	28	29	30			

HABIT REFLECTION

What worked this week?

What didn't? How can you adjust your habit plan or change your experiment for this month?

2022 # OCTOBER

MONDAY
17

TUESDAY
18

WEDNESDAY
19

THURSDAY
20

FRIDAY
21

SATURDAY
22

SUNDAY
23

DON'T FORGET!

OCTOBER 2022

S	M	T	W	T	F	S
						1
2	3	4	5	6	7	8
9	10	11	12	13	14	15
16	17	18	19	20	21	22
$^{23}/_{30}$	$^{24}/_{31}$	25	26	27	28	29

NOVEMBER 2022

S	M	T	W	T	F	S
		1	2	3	4	5
6	7	8	9	10	11	12
13	14	15	16	17	18	19
20	21	22	23	24	25	26
27	28	29	30			

HABIT REFLECTION

What worked this week?

What didn't? How can you adjust your habit plan or change your experiment for this month?

2022 OCTOBER

MONDAY
24

Diwali begins

TUESDAY
25

WEDNESDAY
26

THURSDAY
27

FRIDAY
28

SATURDAY
29

SUNDAY
30

DON'T FORGET!

OCTOBER 2022						
S	M	T	W	T	F	S
						1
2	3	4	5	6	7	8
9	10	11	12	13	14	15
16	17	18	19	20	21	22
23/30	24/31	25	26	27	28	29

NOVEMBER 2022						
S	M	T	W	T	F	S
		1	2	3	4	5
6	7	8	9	10	11	12
13	14	15	16	17	18	19
20	21	22	23	24	25	26
27	28	29	30			

HABIT REFLECTION

What worked this week?

What didn't? How can you adjust your habit plan or change your experiment for this month?

NOVEMBER 2022

SUNDAY	MONDAY	TUESDAY	WEDNESDAY	THURSDAY	FRIDAY	SATURDAY
30	31	1	2	3	4	5
6 Daylight Saving Time ends (USA, CAN)	7	8 Election Day	9	10	11	12
13	14	15	16	17	18 Veterans Day (USA); Remembrance Day (CAN, UK)	19
20	21	22	23	24 Thanksgiving Day	25	26
27	28	29	30 St. Andrew's Day (SCT)	1	2	3

MONTHLY GOALS

What Worked Last Month

What Could Be Better

New Goals to Focus On

"Every choice we make in life is an experiment."

YOUR HABIT LOOP

To track a new habit, the first step is to **identify your routine**. What is the habit you are focusing on for the month? Next, you will want to **experiment with rewards** over the next few weeks and **isolate your cue**. Once you follow the steps laid out in the introduction, you can **make a plan** to change that habit.

 Routine

Experimenting with Rewards

Rewards to test

Write down three words to describe how you are feeling after receiving the reward.

Set an alarm for 15 minutes. Now, are you still craving your old habit?

The identified reward

Isolate your cue

Location

Time

Emotional state

Other people

Preceding action

Have a Plan
What is a new routine that you can implement to change the habit while getting the reward?

Track your habits and watch your progress at a glance by listing some below and coloring in the daily boxes!

HABIT TRACKER

2022 OCTOBER/NOVEMBER

MONDAY
31

Halloween

TUESDAY
1

WEDNESDAY
2

THURSDAY
3

FRIDAY
4

SATURDAY
5

SUNDAY
6

Daylight Saving Time ends (USA, CAN)

DON'T FORGET!

NOVEMBER 2022

S	M	T	W	T	F	S
		1	2	3	4	5
6	7	8	9	10	11	12
13	14	15	16	17	18	19
20	21	22	23	24	25	26
27	28	29	30			

DECEMBER 2022

S	M	T	W	T	F	S
				1	2	3
4	5	6	7	8	9	10
11	12	13	14	15	16	17
18	19	20	21	22	23	24
25	26	27	28	29	30	31

HABIT REFLECTION

What worked this week?

What didn't? How can you adjust your habit plan or change your experiment for this month?

2022 NOVEMBER

MONDAY
7

TUESDAY
8

Election Day

WEDNESDAY
9

THURSDAY
10

FRIDAY
11

Veterans Day (USA); Remembrance Day (CAN, UK)

SATURDAY
12

SUNDAY
13

DON'T FORGET!

NOVEMBER 2022

S	M	T	W	T	F	S
		1	2	3	4	5
6	7	8	9	10	11	12
13	14	15	16	17	18	19
20	21	22	23	24	25	26
27	28	29	30			

DECEMBER 2022

S	M	T	W	T	F	S
				1	2	3
4	5	6	7	8	9	10
11	12	13	14	15	16	17
18	19	20	21	22	23	24
25	26	27	28	29	30	31

HABIT REFLECTION

What worked this week?

What didn't? How can you adjust your habit plan or change your experiment for this month?

2022 NOVEMBER

MONDAY
14

TUESDAY
15

WEDNESDAY
16

THURSDAY
17

FRIDAY
18

SATURDAY
19

SUNDAY
20

DON'T FORGET!

NOVEMBER 2022							**DECEMBER 2022**						
S	M	T	W	T	F	S	S	M	T	W	T	F	S
		1	2	3	4	5					1	2	3
6	7	8	9	10	11	12	4	5	6	7	8	9	10
13	14	15	16	17	18	19	11	12	13	14	15	16	17
20	21	22	23	24	25	26	18	19	20	21	22	23	24
27	28	29	30				25	26	27	28	29	30	31

HABIT REFLECTION

What worked this week?

What didn't? How can you adjust your habit plan or change your experiment for this month?

2022 **NOVEMBER**

MONDAY
21

TUESDAY
22

WEDNESDAY
23

THURSDAY
24

Thanksgiving Day

FRIDAY
25

SATURDAY
26

SUNDAY
27

DON'T FORGET!

NOVEMBER 2022

S	M	T	W	T	F	S
		1	2	3	4	5
6	7	8	9	10	11	12
13	14	15	16	17	18	19
20	21	22	23	24	25	26
27	28	29	30			

DECEMBER 2022

S	M	T	W	T	F	S
				1	2	3
4	5	6	7	8	9	10
11	12	13	14	15	16	17
18	19	20	21	22	23	24
25	26	27	28	29	30	31

HABIT REFLECTION

What worked this week?

What didn't? How can you adjust your habit plan or change your experiment for this month?

DECEMBER 2022

SUNDAY	MONDAY	TUESDAY	WEDNESDAY	THURSDAY	FRIDAY	SATURDAY
27	28	29	30	1	2	3
4	5	6	7	8	9	10
11	12	13	14 Pearl Harbor Day	15	16	17
18 Hanukkah begins	19	20	21 Winter begins (Northern Hemisphere)	22	23	24 Christmas Eve
25 Christmas Day	26 Kwanzaa begins; Boxing Day (AUS, CAN, NZ, UK)	27	28	29	30	31 New Year's Eve

MONTHLY GOALS

What Worked Last Month

What Could Be Better

New Goals to Focus On

"When people believe they are in control, they tend to work harder and push themselves more. They are, on average, more confident and overcome setbacks faster."

YOUR HABIT LOOP

To track a new habit, the first step is to **identify your routine**. What is the habit you are focusing on for the month? Next, you will want to **experiment with rewards** over the next few weeks and **isolate your cue**. Once you follow the steps laid out in the introduction, you can **make a plan** to change that habit.

Routine

Experimenting with Rewards

Rewards to test

Write down three words to describe how you are feeling after receiving the reward.

Set an alarm for 15 minutes. Now, are you still craving your old habit?

The identified reward

Isolate your cue

Location

Time

Emotional state

Other people

Preceding action

Have a Plan
What is a new routine that you can implement to change the habit while getting the reward?

Track your habits and watch your progress at a glance by listing some below and coloring in the daily boxes!

HABIT TRACKER

2022 NOVEMBER/DECEMBER

MONDAY
28

TUESDAY
29

WEDNESDAY
30

St. Andrew's Day (SCT)

THURSDAY
1

FRIDAY
2

SATURDAY
3

SUNDAY
4

DON'T FORGET!

DECEMBER 2022

S	M	T	W	T	F	S
				1	2	3
4	5	6	7	8	9	10
11	12	13	14	15	16	17
18	19	20	21	22	23	24
25	26	27	28	29	30	31

JANUARY 2023

S	M	T	W	T	F	S
1	2	3	4	5	6	7
8	9	10	11	12	13	14
15	16	17	18	19	20	21
22	23	24	25	26	27	28
29	30	31				

HABIT REFLECTION

What worked this week?

What didn't? How can you adjust your habit plan or change your experiment for this month?

2022 DECEMBER

MONDAY
5

TUESDAY
6

WEDNESDAY
7

Pearl Harbor Day

THURSDAY
8

FRIDAY
9

SATURDAY
10

SUNDAY
11

DON'T FORGET!

DECEMBER 2022

S	M	T	W	T	F	S
				1	2	3
4	5	6	7	8	9	10
11	12	13	14	15	16	17
18	19	20	21	22	23	24
25	26	27	28	29	30	31

JANUARY 2023

S	M	T	W	T	F	S
1	2	3	4	5	6	7
8	9	10	11	12	13	14
15	16	17	18	19	20	21
22	23	24	25	26	27	28
29	30	31				

HABIT REFLECTION

What worked this week?

What didn't? How can you adjust your habit plan or change your experiment for this month?

2022 **DECEMBER**

MONDAY
12

TUESDAY
13

WEDNESDAY
14

THURSDAY
15

FRIDAY
16

SATURDAY
17

SUNDAY
18

Hanukkah begins

DON'T FORGET!

DECEMBER 2022
S	M	T	W	T	F	S
				1	2	3
4	5	6	7	8	9	10
11	12	13	14	15	16	17
18	19	20	21	22	23	24
25	26	27	28	29	30	31

JANUARY 2023
S	M	T	W	T	F	S
1	2	3	4	5	6	7
8	9	10	11	12	13	14
15	16	17	18	19	20	21
22	23	24	25	26	27	28
29	30	31				

HABIT REFLECTION

What worked this week?

What didn't? How can you adjust your habit plan or change your experiment for this month?

2022 **DECEMBER**

MONDAY
19

TUESDAY
20

WEDNESDAY
21

Winter begins (Northern Hemisphere)

THURSDAY
22

FRIDAY
23

SATURDAY
24

Christmas Eve

SUNDAY
25

Christmas Day

DON'T FORGET!

DECEMBER 2022							**JANUARY 2023**						
S	M	T	W	T	F	S	S	M	T	W	T	F	S
				1	2	3	1	2	3	4	5	6	7
4	5	6	7	8	9	10	8	9	10	11	12	13	14
11	12	13	14	15	16	17	15	16	17	18	19	20	21
18	19	20	21	22	23	24	22	23	24	25	26	27	28
25	26	27	28	29	30	31	29	30	31				

HABIT REFLECTION

What worked this week?

What didn't? How can you adjust your habit plan or change your experiment for this month?

2022/23 DECEMBER/JANUARY

MONDAY
26

Kwanzaa begins; Boxing Day (AUS, CAN, NZ, UK)

TUESDAY
27

WEDNESDAY
28

THURSDAY
29

FRIDAY
30

SATURDAY
31

New Year's Eve

SUNDAY
1

New Year's Day

DON'T FORGET!

DECEMBER 2022

S	M	T	W	T	F	S
				1	2	3
4	5	6	7	8	9	10
11	12	13	14	15	16	17
18	19	20	21	22	23	24
25	26	27	28	29	30	31

JANUARY 2023

S	M	T	W	T	F	S
1	2	3	4	5	6	7
8	9	10	11	12	13	14
15	16	17	18	19	20	21
22	23	24	25	26	27	28
29	30	31				

HABIT REFLECTION

What worked this week?

What didn't? How can you adjust your habit plan or change your experiment for this month?

YEAR IN REFLECTION

Think back on your year and the habits that you worked on. What was your biggest accomplishment? What habit did you feel like you made the greatest strides with?

You have accomplished a lot this year! It's not easy changing habits that are so ingrained in our everyday lives. What was something that you struggled with the most this year with your habits?

Was it one habit in particular? Or was there a common factor about many of your habits that was hard to change?

What would you like to work on next year? Would you like to continue working on any habits from this year, or are there new ones that you would like to focus on?

NOTES

NOTES

CHARLES DUHIGG is a Pulitzer Prize–winning investigative reporter. He wrote previously for *The New York Times* and now writes for *The New Yorker*. One of his most popular magazine articles—exploring how Target uses data to determine if shoppers are pregnant—was excerpted from *The Power of Habit*. Duhigg has authored multiple series, and was part of the team that won the 2013 Explanatory Pulitzer for "The iEconomy," which explored the impact of Apple's manufacturing in China and the United States.

Duhigg is a graduate of Harvard Business School and Yale University, and a frequent guest on *This American Life*, NPR, *The NewsHour with Jim Lehrer*, *Frontline*, and other programs. Before becoming a journalist, Duhigg worked in private equity and—for one terrifying day—was a bike messenger in San Francisco. He lives in Brooklyn with his wife, a marine biologist, and their two sons.

The Power of Habit spent more than sixty weeks on the *New York Times* bestseller list and has been translated into more than forty languages.

charlesduhigg.com • Facebook.com/charlesduhigg • Twitter: @cduhigg

---

Copyright © 2021 by Charles Duhigg
Written by Charles Duhigg
Original book *The Power of Habit* published by Penguin Random House
Cover and internal design © 2021 Sourcebooks
Cover and internal design by Brittany Vibbert/Sourcebooks
Illustrations by Anton Ioukhnovets

Sourcebooks and the colophon are registered trademarks of Sourcebooks.

All rights reserved. No part of this planner may be reproduced in any form or by any electronic or mechanical means including information storage and retrieval systems—except in the case of brief quotations embodied in critical articles or reviews—without permission in writing from its publisher, Sourcebooks.

All trademarks and copyrights are acknowledged as being the properties of their respective owners and no sponsorship, affiliation, or endorsement is claimed or implied.

Jewish and Muslim holidays begin at sundown.

Published by Sourcebooks
P.O. Box 4410, Naperville, Illinois 60567-4410
(630) 961-3900
sourcebooks.com

Printed and bound in Singapore.
OGP 10 9 8 7 6 5 4 3 2 1

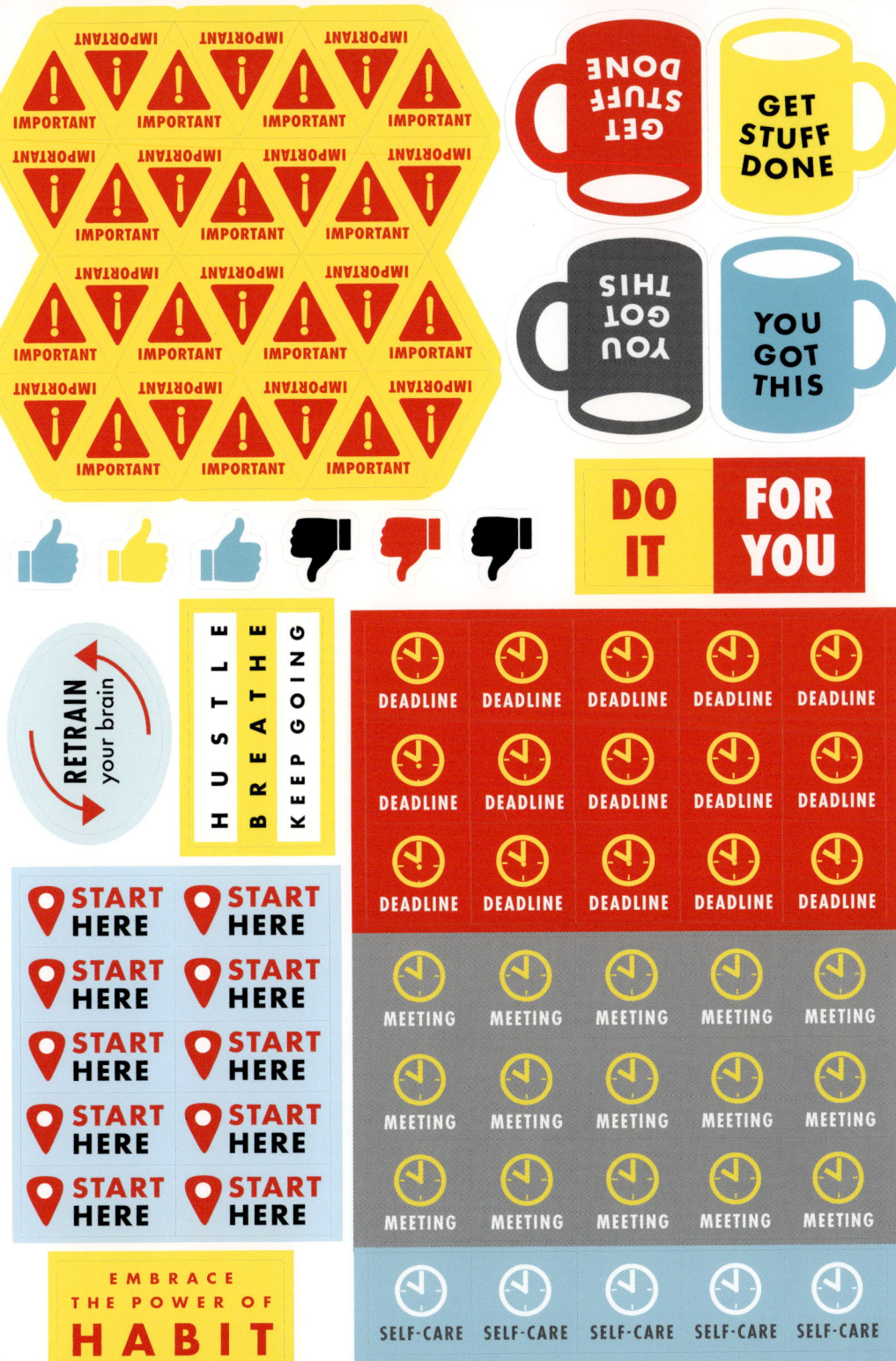

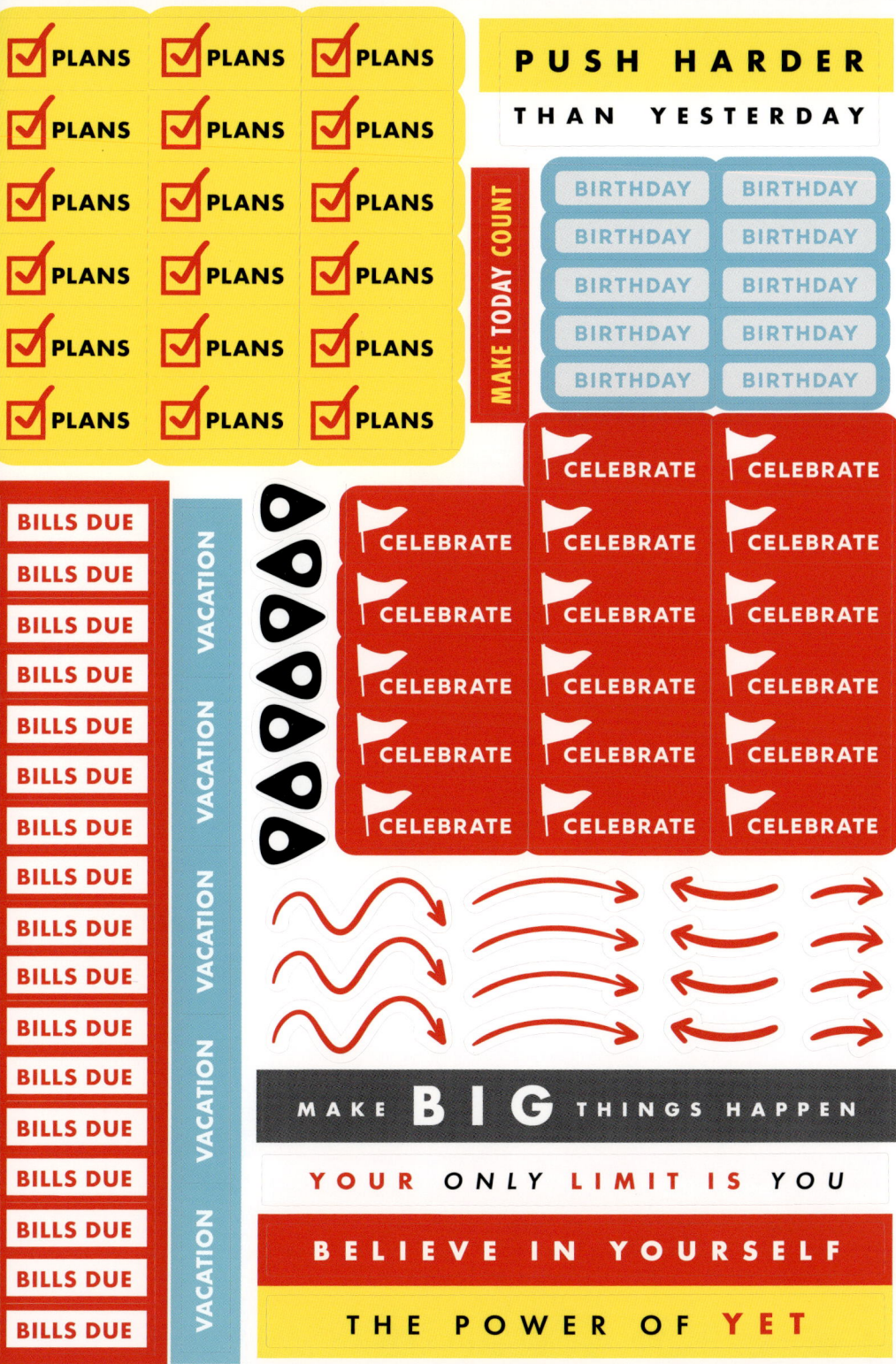